CHRISTOPHER ROUSE

KAROLJU

for SATB Chorus and Orchestra
PIANO/VOCAL SCORE

HENDON MUSIC

BOOSEY & HAWKES

AN IMAGEM COMPANY

DISTRIBUTED BY

HAL•LEONARD®
CORPORATION
7777 W. BLUEMOUND RD. P.O. BOX 13819 MILWAUKEE, WI 53213

www.boosey.com
www.halleonard.com

Two paths led to the composition of *Karolju*. The first was the great body of Christmas carols written over the centuries, a collection I value as highly for its spiritual meaning as for its glorious music. The second was Carl Orff's *Carmina Burana*, which made an unforgettable impression upon me when I first heard it in March of 1963.

In the early 1980s, I conceived of a plan to compose a collection of Christmas carols couched in an overall form similar to that of *Carmina Burana*, but it was not until 1989, when the work was commissioned by the Baltimore Symphony Orchestra, that I was able to begin serious work on it, though I had composed several of the carols in my mind over the preceding years.

As I wished to compose the music first, the problem of texts presented itself. Finding appropriate existing texts to fit already composed music would have been virtually impossible, and as I did not trust my own ability to devise a poetically satisfying text, I decided to compose my own texts in a variety of languages (Latin, Swedish, French, Spanish, Russian, Czech, German, and Italian) which, although making reference to words and phrases appropriate to the Christmas season, would not be intelligibly translatable as complete entities. It was rather my intent to match the sound of the language to the musical style of the carol to which it was applied. I resultantly selected words often more for the quality of their sound and the extent to which such sound typified the language of their origin than for their cognitive "meaning" *per se*.

I also elected to compose music which was direct and simple in its tonal orientation, music which would not seem out of place in a medley of traditional Christmas carols. Those who know other of my works may be surprised – some even distressed – by *Karolju*. While I can assert with assurance that this score does not represent a wholesale "change of direction" for me and thus constitutes an isolated example among my compositions, *Karolju* is nevertheless a piece which I "mean" with the most profound sincerity, one which I hope will help instill in listeners the same special joy which I feel for the season it celebrates.

It has been my decision to eschew complexity or oversubtlety of utterance, preferring instead to compose music as straightforward in terms of melody, harmony, rhythm, and orchestration. Except for a paraphrase of the coda to the "O Fortuna" movements of *Carmina Burana* (which I have used in Nos. 1 and 10 of *Karolju* and which constitutes a small homage to Orff) and for a four-measure phrase in No. 3 which I borrowed from *The Nutcracker* – a phrase which Tchaikovsky himself had cribbed from an eighteenth-century minuet – all of the music in *Karolju* is by me. In an attempt to provide a degree of unity for the work, certain melodic patterns and chord progressions have been employed in a number of the carols.

Karolju was completed in Fairport, New York on November 13, 1990 and is dedicated to my daughter Alexandra, who was to celebrate her first Christmas that year. It was commissioned with the generous assistance of the Barlow Foundation for Music Composition at Brigham Young University, and I am also most grateful to the Guggenheim Foundation for providing me with a Fellowship which allowed me time to compose the work unencumbered by other duties. With a duration of approximately twenty-six minutes, it is scored for large SATB chorus and an orchestra consisting of 2 flutes (2nd doubling piccolo), 2 oboes, 2 clarinets, 2 bassoons, 4 horns, 3 trumpets, 3 trombones, tuba, timpani, percussion (4 players), harp, and strings.

—Christopher Rouse

Piano/Vocal Score

KAROLJU

I.

Words and Music by
CHRISTOPHER ROUSE

979-0-051-32980-9

na-vi-do-rum est, glo-ri-a quo ad Pa-tri-bus rex. Et Fi-li-us

sanc-ti lo-que-tur cum tra-ve-tan-ti sum, es-se ad sta-bit hu-i-us

4

ru - nus te_____ cae - lo de__ mar - cit ad qua,_____ ta - men

ru - nus te_____ cae - lo de__ mar - cit ad qua,_____ ta - men

ru - nus te cae - lo de__ mar - cit ad qua,_____ ta - men

ru - nus te cae - lo de - mar - cit ad_____ qua, ta - men

③

De - o, De - o gra - tias ag - ri - ca - lae

De - o, De - o gra - tias ag - ri - ca - lae

De - o, De - o gra - tias ag - ri - ca - lae

gra - ti - as,_____ De - o gra - ti - as,_____ De - o ag - ri - ca -

6

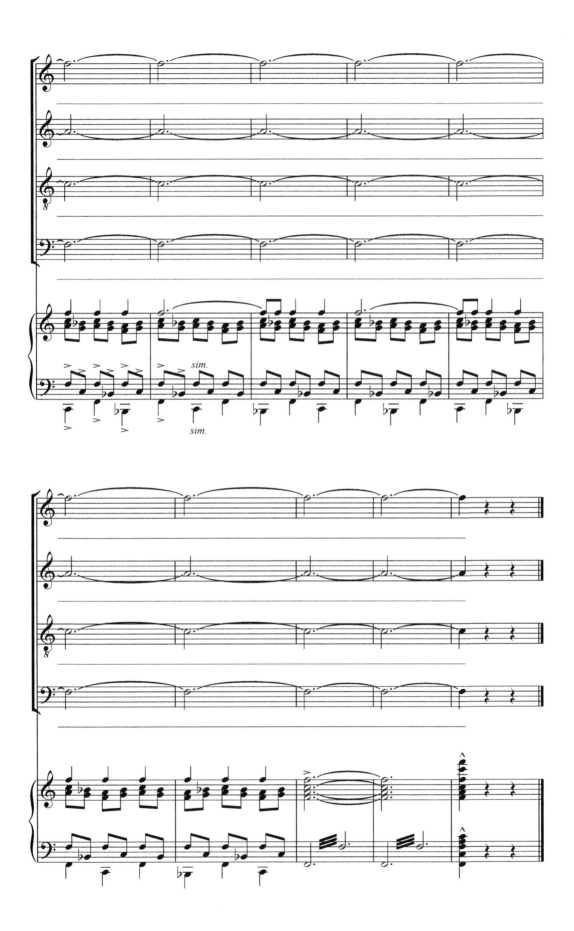

II.

8

12

16

III.

18

20

bé, a ton doux la na - ti - vi - té, la na - ti - vi - té, na - té.

bé, ton doux la na - ti - vi - té, la na - ti - vi - té, la té.

bé, la na - ti - vi - té la na - ti - vi - té la na - ti - vi - té.

bé, la na - ti - vi - té la na - ti - vi - té la na - ti - vi - té.

IV.

V.

VI.

VII.

VIII.

50

54

IX.

60

62

doch emp - fan - den ü - ber an oft aus schla - ge zu, schla - ge zu, schlag.

doch emp - fan - den ü - ber an oft aus zu, schla - ge zu, schla - ge, schlag.

doch emp - fan - den ü - ber an oft schla - ge zu,___ schlag.

doch emp - fan - den ü - ber an oft aus_ schla - ge zu, ja schlag.

O das

das

O das

attacca

X.

73

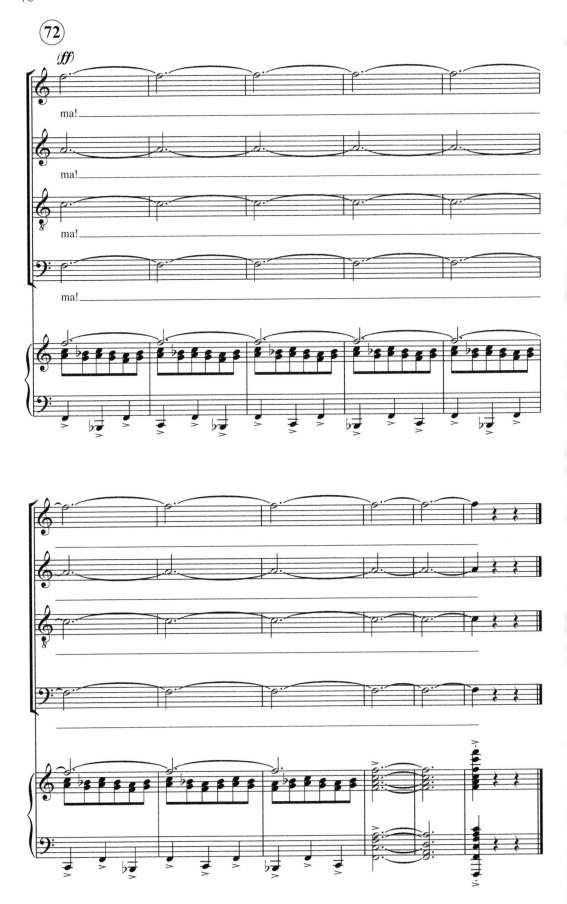

ma! _____

ma! _____

ma! _____

ma! _____

XI.

78

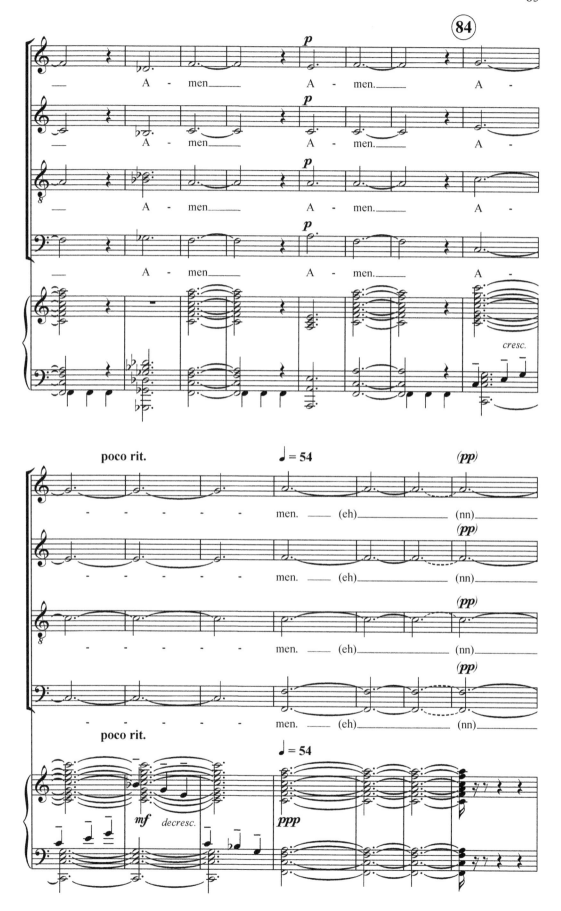